YOUR KNOWLEDGE HAS VALUE

AF148927

- - We will publish your bachelor's and master's thesis, essays and papers

- - Your own eBook and book - sold worldwide in all relevant shops

- - Earn money with each sale

Upload your text at www.GRIN.com and publish for free

Benjamin Renner

Bottom of the pyramid: Doing business with the poor

GRIN Verlag

Bibliografische Information der Deutschen Nationalbibliothek:

Die Deutsche Bibliothek verzeichnet diese Publikation in der Deutschen National-
bibliografie; detaillierte bibliografische Daten sind im Internet über http://dnb.d-
nb.de/ abrufbar.

Dieses Werk sowie alle darin enthaltenen einzelnen Beiträge und Abbildungen
sind urheberrechtlich geschützt. Jede Verwertung, die nicht ausdrücklich vom
Urheberrechtsschutz zugelassen ist, bedarf der vorherigen Zustimmung des Verla-
ges. Das gilt insbesondere für Vervielfältigungen, Bearbeitungen, Übersetzungen,
Mikroverfilmungen, Auswertungen durch Datenbanken und für die Einspeicherung
und Verarbeitung in elektronische Systeme. Alle Rechte, auch die des auszugsweisen
Nachdrucks, der fotomechanischen Wiedergabe (einschließlich Mikrokopie) sowie
der Auswertung durch Datenbanken oder ähnliche Einrichtungen, vorbehalten.

Imprint:

Copyright © 2013 GRIN Verlag GmbH
Druck und Bindung: Books on Demand GmbH, Norderstedt Germany
ISBN: 978-3-656-59477-2

An essay written by a St Andrews postgraduate student at the School of Management based on 'Serving the World's Poor, Profitably' by C.K. Prahalad and Allen Hammond (Harvard Business Review, September 2002) in October 2013.

Introduction

Strive for market shares, the willingness or necessity to increase revenues or diversify risk can be key drivers for innovative firms in going abroad (Peng, 2009). Usually, these companies favour markets somewhat similar to their already developed, saturated home markets with a large potential customer base and mass purchasing power (London & Hart, 2004; Peng, 2009). The article 'Serving the World's Poor, Profitably' written by C.K. Prahalad and Allen Hammond, published in the Harvard Business Review in September 2002, stretches the tremendous sales potential for multi-national enterprises (MNEs) in doing business with the very poor. It builds on the socio-economic concept of the **bottom-of-the-pyramid** (BoP), which refers to nearly four billion potential consumers with an annual income of less than US$ 2,000; that is two-third of the world's population (Prahalad & Hart, 2002).

The authors emphasize the 'untapped potential' (Prahalad & Hammond, 2002: 49) of the aggregated purchasing power of the world's poor that live in rising economies such as Brazil, China, India and South Africa. However, there are many examples for the failure of MNEs in these markets due to prevailing

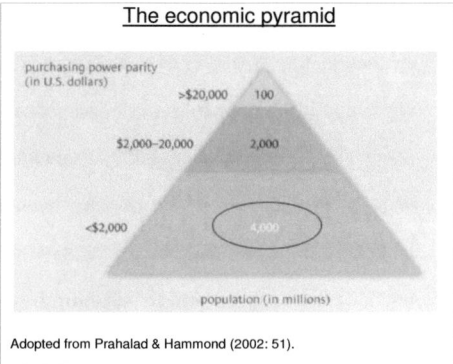

prejudices, substantial misperceptions, and fundamentally flawed strategic decisions. A prominent example of failure is the mobile telecommunications sector (Prahalad & Hammond, 2002; Karnani, 2012). Strategies that are adopted from operations in developed markets often fail when doing business with the poor (Kay & Lewenstein, 2013).

Prahalad's and Hammond's (2002) controversial proposal is that there is no contradiction between making profits when dealing with the poor and improving their living conditions. This will be critically analyzed in more depth hereafter. Since the poor are willing to spend a large portion of their income for non-essential goods, and available products and services are not as cheap as assumed, these markets offer lucrative business opportunities. 'Serving the World's Poor, Profitably' by Prahalad and Hammond is particularly interesting for three reasons; 1) it was published in 2002, which allows a comparison of the key points to be discussed in the light of social progress, 2) the continuing importance of overcoming poverty in today's world (UNDP, 2013) and 3) the strong influence of Prahalad's theses in recent academic discourse in the field of global business strategy (i.e. Yunus, 2008; Karnani, 2012; Simanis, 2012; Kay & Lewenstein, 2013).

Prahalad's and Hammond's theses towards benefits for international businesses

Prahalad and Hammond (2002) state that the four billion poorest people at the base of the economic pyramid represent a lucrative business opportunity for any large multinational enterprise with economies of scale and established supply-chain operations. Even though the definition of the BoP segment or extreme poverty might vary amongst scholars and institutions in terms of purchasing power parity and over time (i.e. Hammond, Kramer, Tran, Katz, Walker, 2007; Prahalad, 2011; UN, 2013), the massive aggregated buying power itself is beyond debate, even though the power in numbers is debatable (Warnholz, 2007). It follows, that MNEs, which have rather targeted the top of the wealth pyramid, can actually **benefit from doing business with the lower tiers of the pyramid** in three ways (Prahalad & Hammond, 2002):

- Growth (revenues)
- Costs (outsourcing, cost structure, efficiency of capital, e-business)
- Innovation (good, services, processes)

2

Growth opportunities in BoP markets eventually result in new revenue streams for the company. The authors specifically refer to the often cited Indian success stories of Citibank Suvidha and Hindustan Lever. The key to success might be to focus on the community instead of individual customers, the so-called 'network-customer' (Prahalad & Hammond, 2002: 52). The high competition on price in these markets requires the MNE to re-build its cost structure in terms of price-performance trade-offs, capital modeling and by making use of IT to eliminate intermediaries. Automatically, companies will come up with new innovations driven by cost pressure and distribution challenges (Prahalad & Hammond, 2002; Prahalad, 2011). Simultaneously, global poverty is reduced, because these companies offer jobs to the local people and provide them with basic goods for consumption (Prahalad & Hammond, 2012). Nevertheless, one could argue that the authors ignore many of the present threats of the markets and limitations for the MNEs.

A study conducted by Monitor Group in India in 2009, cited by Karnani (2012) and Simanis (2012), reveals that only few businesses actually operate profitably in BoP markets. Karnanis' (2012: 9) radical assumption is that 'BOP activities are either profitable but not socially beneficial, or socially virtuous but not profitable'. This might lead to the conclusion that some of the benefits don't exist. In fact, costs for the operation of the business in these markets might be very high (Simanis, 2012). However, it is difficult to discuss Prahalad's and Hammond's theses towards international businesses in more depth, because they are extremely vague in their explanation. When it comes to corporate strategy for BoP market entry, the authors see multiple layers of educating young executives on-site so that they can engage with the poor. Venture funds for investments in local businesses, and departments aiming at identifying and implementing growth opportunities along with the establishment of unconventional partnerships with non-governmental organizations or established companies will help MNEs to effectively manage market entry risk (Prahalad & Hammond, 2002).

A critical discussion of the 'poverty premium'

Even though MNEs may see themselves confronted with **high entry barriers** in the beginning (i.e. inadequate infrastructure, shortage of skilled labour) and a difficult business environment (underground economy), and not least because of legal or political obstacles like complex laws and corruption, it can still be a profitable business for them (Prahalad & Hammond, 2002; London & Hart, 2004; Prahalad, 2011). The reason for this is, that the poor are willing to pay a so-called **'poverty premium'** on everyday goods like loans, phone calls and nutrition, as scientifically proven by the authors in India and elsewhere (Prahalad & Hammond, 2002: 52). The authors trace this back to infrastructural inefficiency and disadvantages of economies of scale with which companies are confronted in slums and rural areas of BoP markets (Prahalad & Hart, 2002). Not only the 'poverty premium' that can be charged compared to middle-class consumers, but also the world's poor brand-consciousness, the on-going urbanization trend and the poor's demand for 'luxury' goods represent great opportunities for organizational creativity (Prahalad & Hammond, 2002; Prahalad 2011).

Since there is still a lack of reliable research about the poor in many emerging countries, the idea of the 'poverty premium' is highly debatable. Others argue it is morally questionable from a company point of view (Mittal & Wallach, 2004) or rather prefer to speak about a 'poverty penalty' (Warnholz, 2007: 3). Interestingly, Hammond et. al. (2007: 16) also use this wording instead of poverty premium. In January 2013, Kay & Lewenstein (2013) conducted research in Dharavi and Warden Road in Mumbai, the same districts that were analyzed by Prahalad and Hammond ten years earlier, and concluded that the concept of the 'poverty premium' does not prove to be true (anymore). In fact, they found some evidence for a 'poverty discount' (Kay & Lewenstein, 2013: 22). One of the reasons for this is the prevailing informal economy with local vendors that offer cheap substitute goods. These vendors aren't regulated by environmental, labour or tax laws and therefore often much more competitive than international firms (London & Hart, 2004; Kay & Lewenstein, 2013).

4

From this it follows, that MNEs willing to address the BoP need to be aware of their real competitive environment. This environment includes retailers from the informal sector that operate under conditions of 'near perfect competition' (Kay & Lewenstein, 2013: 23), which affects the enforceable price spectrum. According to Simanis (2012), who is skeptical about Prahalad's and Hammond's model, MNEs should rather sell at high prices while trying to minimize their variable cost structure. A bad infrastructure in rural areas and missing expertise of the world's poor in regard to consumption results in high fixed costs and risk. This requires market penetration rates of up to 30% in order to operate profitably (Simanis, 2012). He suggests that the same strategy which MNEs use to tackle the peak of the pyramid is more appropriate (Simanis, 2012). However, similar to Karnani (2012), Prahalad and Hammond (2002: 54) emphasize the importance of the internet, which allows to 'eliminate the need for layers of intermediaries'.

The role of the private sector in fighting poverty

Undoubtedly, the vicious cycle of poverty cannot be broken solely by MNEs investing in developing markets. It requires investments in education or the access to health care (UNDP, 2013). It needs informed consumers (Prahalad & Hart, 2002). It requires new partnerships alliances between governments, corporations, non-governmental organizations and international institutions like World Bank, International Monetary Fund and United Nations (London & Hart, 2004). Prahalad and Hammond (2002) don't neglect that. While the traditional view suggests the poor can't help themselves, their market-based approach recognizes the BoP population as consumers (Hammond et. al., 2007). This 'can help frame the debate on poverty reduction more in terms of enabling opportunity and less in terms of aid' (Hammond et.al., 2007: 6), because aid is not sustainable (Prahalad, 2011). Companies need to be profitable when addressing the poor, because otherwise their success will not be sustainable over time (Prahalad & Hammond, 2002). There must be a 'democratization of commerce' (Prahalad, 2011: 20), which points towards a more inclusive form of capitalism.

Interestingly, some of Prahalad's and Hammond's (2002) ideas on the role of the private sector in the fight against poverty have meanwhile been incorporated in the United Nations Development Programme (UNDP, 2009).

But shouldn't doing business with the BoP be part of a firms' global responsibility, a moral obligation, which needs to be integrated in their business model, resulting from their **corporate self-understanding**? Even though many follow Prahalad's arguments, some criticize the message as too ambiguous. Yunus (2008: 2) argues: 'I feel uncomfortable […], because the very attitude tells you, or promotes your idea that you can make money down there'. For example, shouldn't pharmaceutical corporations still operate in developing countries, even though they can't earn money? Of course, CEOs have to act in the best interests of the company and its shareholders, but the poor shouldn't be exploited. Unfortunately, according to Karnani (2012), this seems to be inevitable when the cost structure needs to be revised radically, even though such cost reductions might be achieved with technological inventions. This holds as particularly true since many poor countries are also heavily indebted (IMF, 2013) and often lack strong governments that can guarantee a legal framework for fair business practice (London & Hart, 2004; Karnani, 2012). The view suggested by Prahalad and Hammond in 2002 is very much on what can be sold, namely low-priced high-quality goods like shampoo, instead of what the people at the bottom-of-the-pyramid really need (Karnani, 2012).

The underlying discussion

The economies of many emerging markets are growing more rapidly than ever before (The Economist, 2013). While the Eurozone reports low one-digit GDP growth figures and is said to be hauled out of recession (Eurostat, 2013), and the United States of America ended the political debate about raising the country's debt ceiling for now (REUTERS, 2013), the growth potential of the emerging markets and its population is still huge (Prahalad, 2011).

Above all, scholars agree that unmet needs have to be addressed in these regions (i.e. Mittal & Wallach, 2004; Hammond et.al., 2007; Yunus, 2008; Prahalad, 2011). A large part of the BoP population doesn't have access to drinking-water, sanitation facilities and basic health care (UNDP, 2013). They also don't have proper access to the banking system (Hammond et.al., 2007). Therefore, existing resources must be used utilized efficiently by all means (Stiglitz, 2011). According to Prahalad and Hammond (2002) there might be ground for optimism that a win-win situation for the private sector and the world's poor alike is achievable; profits for the already wealthy MNEs and a decent standard of living for the poor. But does **globalization** really help the poor? This is hard to believe considering the fact that the inequality in income has increased in our world and hundreds of millions of people are undernourished or starving. Child mortality rates are reported to be far above 10% in many African countries (UNDP, 2013). The West was even confronted with massive anti-globalization movements in the last two decades (Stiglitz, 2011). Being directly confronted with such critics as Mittal and Wallach (2004), Prahalad and Hammond (2004: 9) admit that 'globalization has not yet brought many benefits to the poor'. In the course of this discussion, Karnani (2012: 8) criticizes the lack of 'socially useful goods' that MNEs offer to the poor and gives tobacco and alcohol as negative examples.

However, the aforementioned report of the United Nations Development Programme also describes a declined inequality between the high developed and low developed countries in regard to health and education (UNDP, 2013). Moreover, the set targets of the first UN Millennium Development Goal for 2015 related to the eradication of extreme poverty and hunger have been achieved, despite the 2008 financial crisis (UN, 2013). Undoubtedly, much still has to be done. According to the UN (2013) 1.2 billion people around the world are considered to be living in extreme poverty. Prahalad (2011: 138) is optimistic that the 'elimination of poverty and deprivation [is] possible by 2020', while others are more skeptical (i.e. The Economist, 2013). Whether or not the world's poor benefit from globalization might be difficult to answer, but since the publication of Prahalad's and Hammond's article in 2002, impressive progress has been made. Today's world is much more connected and interdependent, not least due to technological advances (Prahalad, 2011). Still, one could argue that Prahalad and Hammond only address income poverty in absolute terms and neglect other non-monetary levels of poverty (Mittal & Wallach, 2004). The upside is that poverty in developing countries also affects the more developed countries, which leads to action.

Conclusion

Overall, Prahalad's and Hammond's article 'Serving the World's Poor, Profitably' is still a must-read in 2013. It is one of the first articles on the bottom-of-the-pyramid by Prahalad, a concept which was originally developed by Prahalad and Stuart L. Hart in 'The Fortune at the Bottom of the Pyramid' earlier in 2002. This article mainly builds on empirical evidence of a 'poverty premium', which the authors found in India. Moreover, it is very concise in its proposition, which allows the reader to critically reflect on it. This is particularly relevant, because recent BoP literature increasingly suggests alternative methods to Prahalad's and Hammond's (2002) recommended business strategy of low-price, high-quality goods and brand-new research even puts Prahalad's and Hammond's so-called 'poverty premium' at a question (Kay & Lewenstein, 2013).

References

Eurostat, (2013, August 14) 'Flash estimate for the second quarter of 2013'. *(Eurostat Press Office)*, Available: http://epp.eurostat.ec.europa.eu/cache/ITY_PUBLIC/2-14082013-AP/ EN/2-14082013-AP-EN.PDF (Accessed: 2013, October 16).

Hammond, A.; Kramer, W.J.; Tran, J.; Katz, R.; Walker C. (2007) *The Next 4 Billion*. Washington: World Resources Institute & International Finance Corporation.

IMF, (2013) 'Debt Relief Under the Heavily Indebted Poor Countries (HIPC) Initiative'. *(International Monetary Fund Communications Department)*, Available: http://www.imf.org /external/np/exr/facts/pdf/hipc.pdf (Accessed: 2013, October 12).

Karnani, A. (2012) 'Markets of the Poor: Opportunities and Limits'. *International Journal of Rural Management,* 8 (1&2): 7-17.

Kay, E. & Lewenstein, W. (2013) 'The Problem with the "Poverty Premium"'. *Harvard Business Review,* 91 (4): 21-23.

London, T. & Hart, S.L. (2004) 'Reinventing Strategies for Emerging Markets: Beyond the Transnational Model'. *Journal of International Business Studies*, 35 (5): 350-370.

Mittal, A., Wallach, L.; Prahalad, C.K. & Hammond, A. (2004) 'Selling Out the Poor'. *Foreign Policy*, (144): 6-10.

Peng, M.W. (2009) *Global Strategic Management 2nd International ed.* South-Western Cengage Learning.

Peng, M.W., Wang, D.Y.L. & Jiang, Y. (2008) 'An institution-based view of international business strategy: a focus on emerging economies'. *Journal of International Business Studies*, 39 (5): 920-936.

Prahalad C.K. (2011) *The Fortune at the Bottom of the Pyramid: Eradicating Poverty Through Profits, Revised and Updated 5th Anniversary ed.* Wharton School Publishing.

Prahalad, C.K. & Hammond, A. (2002) 'Serving the World's Poor, Profitably'. *Harvard Business Review,* 80 (9): 48-57.

Prahalad, C.K. & Hart, S.L. (2002) 'The Fortune at the Bottom of the Pyramid'. *Strategy+Business,* 8 (26): 54-67.

REUTERS, (2013, October 16) 'At 11th hour, U.S. edges away from brink of debt crisis' *(Thomsen Reuters)*, Available: http://uk.reuters.com/article/2013/10/16/uk-usa-fiscal-idUKBRE9970RX20131016 (Accessed: 2013, October 17).

Simanis, E. (2012) 'Reality Check at the Bottom of the Pyramid'. *Harvard Business Review*, 90 (6): 120-125.

Stiglitz, J.E., (2011) 'The Globalization of Protest'. *(Project Syndicate)*, Available: http://www.project-syndicate.org/commentary/stiglitz144/English (Accessed: 2013, October 14).

The Economist, (2013) 'Towards the end of poverty'. *The Economist Newspaper Limited*, 8838 (407): 11.

UN, (2013, July 1) 'The Millennium Development Goals Report'. *(United Nations New York)*, Available: http://un.org/millenniumgoals/pdf/report-2013/mdg-report-2013-english.pdf (Accessed: 2013, October 10).

UNDP, (2009) 'Revised Guidelines on Cooperation between UNDP and the Private Sector'. *(United Nations Development Programme)*, Available: http://business.un.org/en/assets */a33fdc95-4761-48e5-b7cf-c264bc594926* (Accessed: 2013, October 12).

UNDP, (2013) 'Human Development Report 2013 - The Rise of the South: Human Progress in a Diverse World'. *(United Nations Development Programme)*, Available: http://hdr.undp.org/en/media/HDR_2013_EN_complete.pdf (Accessed: 2013, October 12).

Warnholz, J.-L. (2007) 'Poverty Reduction for Profit? A critical examination of business opportunities at the Bottom of the Pyramid'. *Queen Elizabeth House Working Paper Series, University of Oxford.* No. 160.

Yunus, M. (2008, August 29) Interviewed by: Visser, W. *Cambridge Programme for Sustainable Leadership, University of Cambridge.* Available from: http://www.cpsl.cam.ac.uk/Resources/Videos/~/media/Files/Resources/Top%2050%20Su st%20Books/Wayne%20Visser%20video%20transcripts/Cambridge_Interview_Muhamm ad_Yunus_29_08_2008.ashx (Accessed: 2013, October 10).